THE DAKINI CODEX

NICOLE PERSONETTE

ISBN 979-8-88644-182-6 (Paperback)
ISBN 979-8-89112-840-8 (Hardcover)
ISBN 979-8-88644-183-3 (Digital)

Covenant Books
11661 Hwy 707
Murrells Inlet, SC 29576
www.covenantbooks.com

CONTENTS

THE PEN IS MIGHTIER
THAN THE SWORD

The pen is mightier than the sword
Through written word, laws were born
And through the word spoken above
A record of divine love.

The pen is mightier than the sword
Words cast spells when sworn
And through the grammar and syntax given
The inversions upright from heaven
Set the laws in stone.

The pen is mightier than the sword
Upon the removal, a throne was born
Camelot reigned
Its place ordained
From the removal of the sword from stone.

And so it's promised in Divine Law
The sword would be cast into the plow
And from the harvest all will bow

The pen is mightier than the sword.

G.E.N.E.S.I.S.

G is for Genesis, marking the beginning of time.
E encompasses everything, and everything will be fine.
N is for nothing when everything is found.
I is for intrinsically intuitive, and in it you will ground.
S is for spiritual. You have it in spades.
I is for intelligent, for the wisdom you gave.
S is for special. There is no one like you!

Genesis, I am so glad the world has found you!
You pray with the faith of exercised saints.
You overcame obstacles and made it in God's way.
There was never a person who had a bigger heart.
The lives you touch are golden, and to them you will impart
A new and improved way of looking at life.
You will make the hearts of others blossom
     with your faith made alive.
An angel that graced us will be called
Genesis, this beginning, whose heart knew it all.

THE SHROUD OF TURIN

Yeshua Hamashiach came
The ark of the covenant reign
The Shroud of Turin maimed
The living bloodstain.
And many in their demise
Cast lots over the Turin shrine
And covered over the life benign
And claimed it for their own line.
The Holy Grail toasted the cup
Was it O negative boiling up?
To keep the controllers stationed topped
Upon the golden throne did bind.
Little did they know, the rose
That set the flowering growth of glow
And so that was humbled deep below
The AB negative in mine.
And so the stories made of old
Transmute the mourning that cast the gold
And with a mark of Cain be told
All that came in time.
I carried both in this vessel
The sorcerer's stone of alchemical lessons
Transmute the sphere of Amenti tresses
From shining red to heart green rolled
For the sake of earth's ascension
Source code fail-safe and all its measures
A golden portal link of treasures
Between the braided threefold cord

With living waters I set up to bind
The fractured sections of the realm in time
And sacred geometry's eternal life find
Blossoms in the center of thine
Inside it I hold the keys of heaven
And set it away from the cast of seven
Return it now like the bread causes leaven
To allow its best to rise.
And so it is in the *I Am* presence
My gift to mankind to know its resonance
And live the wholly of holy's presents
To know the love that births existence
In this sacred heart of mine.

LOVE IS

Love is true-hearted and unselfishly kind
And bears the circumstances of trying times.
Love believes all things with hope so strong.
Love never fails and can never go wrong.

Love is faith, the epitome of God,
And through love's reflection, our self-interests are shod.
Love is forgiving and rejoices with good,
Love is believing that circumstances could.
Change with time when love is mine.,
True love is there for you.
For love, it gives, refines, and sieves.
All the past we leave behind,
All the pain that is in our minds.
Love is infinite through time.

AWAKENING PRAYER

The morning mist envelops me
And encompasses a prismed light.
The sun grounds and surrounds me
As my soul is taken to a different height.
I hear the whispers of Mother Earth.
Her maternal instincts call
Under the watchful eye
Of Father Sky.
I'm surrounded by it all.
The gentle breath of rolling fog,
The birds that awaken with a song,
A frozen moment may not last that long,
But inside me is preserved alive.
I raise my hands to the Father Sky,
And ask for strength under his watchful eye
That even if my life should go awry,
I'll be safe inside His arms.

JE T'AIME

Your love is the feeling of becoming one with heaven.
It is to touch the clouds and know freedom at last.
It is the starlight sky brought down to earth
        to play inside the forest canopy.
It is the echo of a breathtaking cathedral.
The pristine shine of a thousand icicles.
It is addicting as sweet wine, and as lips that long to be kissed.

And if love cannot bring us these presents,
        just as I give these gifts to you,
It will feel like a sting that dwells deep inside this heart
Until the tears fall down my cheeks like passionate rivers.

For I have known in my mind and felt in my heart
        that it is your love I shall thirst for.
And it is your love I shall need to survive.

UNSPOKEN WORDS

They say the eyes are a window to the soul.
I was just gazing into these limpid pools
And with this hand you've given me.
You gaze with a different sight.
This love offer that surrounds me
As these unspoken words take flight.
I trace your face with my hands
As if to remember your gaze.
Like it would be etched in my mind
On a carved granite interface.
I feel your love from the aura of your heart.
That magnificent grove that never seeks to part.
This gentle embrace in breath of sighs
Places me on a lover's high.
The sincerity of your eyes encased in tears
Holds the promise of a million years.
These unspoken words that lie unfurled
Speak louder than one may say.
In stillness it is held with time
And never washes away.

ON YOUR TENTH
WEDDING ANNIVERSARY

Love is a crown of royalty
In the sheer essence of its loyalty,
Endowed upon its regal glow
In the dreams of love here below—
A collage of beautiful memories.

When true love grows,
It infinitely shows
In all its miraculous ways,
For it becomes so young
Never leaves unsung
It's love for all its days.

With the passage of time,
It embellishes like wine
And becomes more refined
Like a blossoming rose.
For love never fades
Never counts all its days,
And time becomes all of its own.

ROSE

A lover's blush
A bouquet of blooms
A summer's rush
Of pink hues.
A flavor that mingles
In long-legged strains.
The cork's aroma that wrinkles
The nose of great gain.
It warms the cheeks
Like it warms the heart.
A gift to you my love,
Cheers to a great start!

TO BE YOUNG

To see the world through the eyes of a child.
To dance on clouds all whispered and wild.
To derive a thousand words from one single picture.
And to see mankind as a colorful mixture.
To realize your dreams are all within reach.
To experience life, to learn, and to teach.
To give nothing a reason for me to grow bitter,
Or lose its luster color and wither.

For this is what it means for me to be young:
To never let hopes and dreams go unsung,
And so after all is said and is done,
I will have known what it meant for me to be young.

To see moonlight dance from wave to shore
To be content with life and not ask for more.
To find solace and pleasure in the first fallen snow
And to find joy and fulfillment in watching things grow.

For this is what it means for me to be young:
To never let love and life go unsung,
And so after all is said and is done,
I will have known what it meant for me to be young.

MY LOVE

My love is an abyss that is overwhelmingly deep
Love could get lost in it.

My love is an aged liquor
That embellishes and intoxicates.

My love is intense.

So much love I could give until you have drunken
	your fill, you could no longer stand it.

My love is a ripe flower—fragile and ready.

My love is towering, as infinite as a starlight sky.

Yet my love is critical. My love could grow
	in minutes, die in minutes.
All I have known is exquisite pain. Pain near
	death but not entirely disillusioned.
Pain in which no poet nor judge could justify.

My love is secretive, intimate. My love can replace pain with
	hopes. My love can be spiritual, healing everything.

My love is intense.

Everything I have to give is in my power to love. It is
theatrical, dramatic, poetic, and romantic.

My love is your love, and your love is mine. And it is no
less than everything to you, to me. Always.

SOUL SHINE

With the brilliance of a thousand stars
And galaxies that collide in the warmth of your eyes,
I see the universe in you that creates my awareness
A mirror reflection of worlds that crashed into mine.
Whole kingdoms and ages of time
Enter into the inner sanctum of my heart.
And through these words need not depart,
I see your soul shine.

My brother and sister who have joined me in this journey,
Living on earth to change our past
And bring forth our future that is meant to last.
I must step out from my long-lost rest
To know my higher self at best
And align myself with growth of learning
In order to see my soul shine.

May all be revealed in divine time,
These twists and turns,
Victories and burns.
These tears and sorrows we grind.
I transmute and bend
And practice over again
In order to see our souls shine.

TWIN FLAMES

My twin flame
The soul's same
Call my name
To you I came
A mirror image
I saw myself
In your rummage
Reached out to help
On the line of scrimmage
My heart melts
Set on fire
My soul ascends
My passion lit
My lover friend
Our connection birthed
On a plane
Beset by distance
It's all the same
I feel your presence
Your fire rages
Burn into reverence
The Goddess flame
I scream your name
My body melts
I drift to sleep
The dreams of you
My heart songs keep
Until the day

You come my way
And in me play
To come what may
The lover's game
I call your name
Just like a prayer
And with this beat
To know no repeat
This attraction is like a soothsayer.

THESE GIFTS OF LOVE

These tokens of love
The full moon and shining sun
Starlight to hang upon my veil
To encompass and surround me
Light shining all around me
In cosmic force, these things sound
Its creation and its breaking ground
From source code, it measures grand and loud
These token gifts of love.

In my hand on finger lies
A diamond crystal to catch the eye
A token gift caught up on high
To adorn my lover's heart.

And on my bed red petals lie
Fill the air with a gentle sigh
I lay my head down on this bed
To my lover's room I am wed.

This embrace that encompasses the soul
Wrapped in angel wings of feather touch
I breathe slowly as I go
These token gifts of true love.

TANTRA

Weaving through this moment of time,
Your timelines crash into mine.
They emerge a new beginning
In tantric line of ebb and flow.
My life exodus through you.
And in this energy that encompasses all that may be,
I feel it move inside of me
As if our physical bodies collided.
Like a supernova in the sky,
I abide in the starry night,
And my soul is emerged as one.
Our lives create to have begun.
All this that lived in heart, mind, and soul.
And so it is with every newborn goal.
The thought of you conceived with cosmic force.
Creates the universe of our very existence.
We become one.
And so it is, and so it is.
Beloved I am, and so it is.

TO THOSE WITHOUT PITY

"Cruel of heart, lay down my song
Your reading eyes have done me wrong…"

For you were told by many that I did not care.
Ceaseless love now desensitized there.
Without a word, I see you pass.
Your mind erect, your eyes as glass.
Not a single tear or phrase for me?
So was it time that set you free?
A dreamless boy so filled with passion
Left my throat still dry and my love still questioned.
The needs of love in anguish past
Made me think this love would last.
A death of heart, a bloody rose,
Withers as the summer goes
So love will always fade.
But with strength renewed and dreams renewed,
I'll wait for you this day.

I KNOW

I know what you wanted to say is going to please me.
I know what you might do that will make me cry.
I know what will happen in the near future,
But I am also afraid to ask why.

This hope tears at my heart strings
For this long-awaited dream.
For all my childhood memories are now foreshadowed and gleamed.
I know what you want to relate lies deep within your soul
And tears from within you to reach this very goal.
The words are yearning at the tip of your tongue
And at the same time destroyed you and stung.

I know you'll cross every ocean.
You'll find your way through the storm
To find the peace of mind from your pain
And relief of the weight you've born.

I'm with you in the ocean.
I'm fighting my way through the storm.
I'm crossing my pain to relieve the weight I've born.

I love you for your struggling fight,
I'll accept you for your painful plight.
I'll show you new horizons,
The wonderful things you have to gain.
I'll turn all that is insane sane.
I'll turn all those prison walls

That leave you cold and gray
And fill it with the words you long for me to say.
I'll make a temple with all your art
And fill it with gold, silver, and stars.
I'll teach you the essence of my soul
In every form, way, sound, and goal.

There is so much that this love can do,
It knows no bounds for nourishing you.

FEELINGS

Depression roams like a drifting tide
Happiness will lack and a smile will hide
A tearing inside of flesh and of soul
A feeling of failure to a particular goal.

Pride, however, on the other hand
Tries to be held yet blows like sand
Pride may be uplifting to many of those
But leads to a failure of a particular mode.

A giving expression is not like depression
It has nothing to do with pride
A smile will grin as a friendship begins
When a giving expression cannot hide.

THIS HEART OF MINE

Shattered and tattered and ragged for wear.
Busted and battered, burned and bare.
Tired yet wired and restless in cares.
Broken of tokens in heart and wares.
I see you, I feel you, I hurt as you do.
I need you, the real you, and the worst that you knew.
It hurt me, it swerved me, it made me stew.
It revived me, it enlivened me, this heart of
        mine and from that I knew.
In this moment of time, my heart was not mine.
It began to chime; for it had been true.

INSIDE OF ME

Within the quiet of my monkey mind
The chatter in my brain
The constant talk and egoic balk
That makes me feel insane
Is a spaciousness that exist
Its birthing place that now persists
To destroy the voice that resists
Within this moment of time.

Cycling along the breath work
Where the soul is closed and scared
I open my lungs to take the air
This practiced intent to calm the fear
Among this creative year
So that with vision I may steer
My shadow self that creeps and lurks.

And so with integration I try
An acceptance of all murk left behind
So that in conscious forms I find
A peace within my soul.

A transition in knowing that all things change
And suffering that feels so strange
The tears to sort out all this pain
Can transmute the growth of range.

As each group cycles closer than last
In spirals of pain body's past
I grow stronger with every weighted mask
And so it is with every task
To destroy the suffering of my soul.

TO TRAVEL THE
ROAD LESS TAKEN

I walk the path less traveled,
Full of brimstone and ash
And have seen my share of trials battled,
Feeling like sharp, cold edges of shattered glass.

I've traveled the road less taken,
Then others have dared to walk
Or others even care to hear of
When people care to talk.

I've journeyed the road less used
That many have come to neglect,
Although the truth of the matter is,
It is not so easy to forget.

The path of the road less taken
Others have taken too,
And many have experienced that road
Of the battered and the bruised.

It may seem like you are alone
When it is you against the world.
When no one cares to know about
The footsteps you have tread
To realize the survival of the spirit
And to make all come alive, which was dead
Is to walk the road less traveled.

A VICTORY OF COST

To search for you intently and know just how you feel,
As tears well in this aching heart, questioning what is real.
So I follow in your footsteps of times that we have lost
And wonder if I will see you
A victory of cost!
As I build myself a fantasy
Of loves that I have lost.
Again I ponder victory
But only that of cost.

For the love I hold so dearly
Is held with all my heart
And dangles with the string
Of a never-ending part.
My love for you is the ocean,
Which crashes in the storm
And carries your affection
I thought that you had born.

These precious memories are all that I possess,
Given me through time in an excruciating test.
So, a victory of cost loving can sometimes be,
A questioning of time and a wonderment of me!

JOE THE BARTENDER

Joe, the bartender with a pirate's eye patch and a tasseled tall tail
And a bartender's visor that glistens a green veil
His signature drink, Southern Comforts, at best
From the deep South Carolina from Camden's great rest
He started his days as a lonely little pup
Tied to the tree of a yawning live oak
And so it began, the days of this bloke
His sentinel guard looks on with a toke
And says to the girl who showed up at the shop
"We don't sell the pup here," and that was all that she got
So she left that day with a twinkle in her eye
"I'll break him out of the clink the next time I stop by"
Known from her friends as Squeaky, she rode
To take the young pup from the place he was stowed
In the rear of the car and brought swiftly he rode
Through the back routes to a horse show he towed
And found a New England lady to finally unload
And make his place in his new Keswick home.
Step up to the bar, what's your story you brought
Are you a rescue from the life you have sought?
Do you have the blues while you drink your last draught?
What blew you in to the tie in the tree?
What caused your pirate's patch and the things you did see?
Does it change the way now you are looking at me?
The tap-danced great caper to finally be free?
I tell my tale as I hand you a drink
The spirits set sail, and the sadness did sink
I am Joe the bartender, as sly as a mink

And I give you a wave and send you a wink
Be the hero to gauge your great story and think
You can be a rescue from the lonely old clink
And set yourself free as you step up to the brink
I set myself free and I give you this link.

GAS LIGHTING FIRES

This byzantine maze of smoke and mirrors,
Mists of haze and alabaster quivers
Shoot from directions that boggle the mind.
I tread in dark water, but in the light, I find
This battle is not mine.
Within grounding I am centered,
I see you with pitied sight.
I shield myself from painful words
In an aura of white light.
I release this twitching eye
And pain in my lower back.
This disease you spread on high
With your verbal attack.
I acknowledged what I could change,
But still it was not enough.
To see you manipulate your rage
In what you think is love roughed up.
The compliment the soul
And punch it as you go
And think this is where passion is lit
Leaves me crying over what you did.
It dims your sacred light.
How sad that within you finds
Judgment in dual mind.
In this you fight your own room of smoke and mirrors.
In my knowing, I am bestowed
That whatever said is also felt within.
While your finger points with sharp words

Three steal your heart with swords.
I would like to reassure you that my kindness is not an act.
But this final curtain is lowered, and there is no turning back.
These gas lighting fires I extinguish in love.
I pray every day for this to retire.
These diseased words and gas lighting fires.

THE SOUNDS OF SILENCE

When an answer is made
That doesn't reflect the heart it gave
When an explanation said
Feels the weighted heart of dread.

I seek the sounds of silence.

In the knowing deep within
The answers given inside I send
Each response that I may say
Doesn't carve to find a way
In the bridge that seeks forming
Crumbles with the sounds that are storming.

I find myself in the sounds of silence.

And so the path spirals inside
Because the answer always hides
In this knowing, I abide
And in these answers that I find
Reveal the answers that I seek
And matches the desire that is meek
Calms the storm that does abide
In these answers deep inside.

I hear the sounds of silence.

And so I begin to let go
Of all that doesn't allow the flow
And in these echoes deep below
The wells of laughter and talk bestow

The sounds of silence.

CHOICE

A choice that was taken
Created a forsaken
Measure of increments
That destroy the home
In overlooking right path
With no middle way
No medium of virtue
Was able to stay
And now the crack made
In quantum energy gave
A split in time
Where severance creates
A falling away
With vortex spirals
Line in rhymes
Of energy rivals
And now began
A letting go of trials
A severance of ego
In trisula strikings
In quantum creation
Of Dakini measures
In a light language tongues
Of portal treasures
Now strikes the dance
Its viral measures
On top of the cosmos
In radiant spaces

I am the enigma
The stipulation of stigma
The destroyer of dogma
And the wheel of karma
While in the wheel of dharma
The turns with life
And anti-life matters
That brought in strife
The choices were marked
Created by heart
And the quantum universe
Now traverses
The parallel lines
That crosses through times
And brings in the rays
Across solar rhymes
It's calling, it's calling
The flash for the balling
The light all enthralling
Is coming in time
From choices from choices
The heart gives the voices
The Lotus-born Master
Then comes to rise.

JUST WORDS

When words that are said are not followed by action
When intent of heart is not given pure traction
When faces come and go like blurs in the wind
And no meaning is given to the spirits they send
It is just mere words spoken
No meaning, no token
No real genuine measure
Of golden heart treasure
No life in work where words only fail
To concepts and dreams that are forced down to hail
When integrity and dignity do not have a meaning
Because lackluster qualities come in a streaming
When no consistency is given, and frustration runs high
Because words that are spoken are not acted as nigh
And allowance for mediocrity begins
Is a destroyer of morals and an unforgivable sin
When mandates mask the spirit of God
Despite being peaceable, no respect is shod
A fading away of presence will be
The estate left desolate for all to see
A home without life is a dead place to me
Without heart, without words that back actions to be.

THROUGH THE TWO-WAY MIRROR

Through the two-way mirror
I see myself
Separated as a human and the awareness mind
I envision the recollection
And its reflection
Of the current in the now moment of time
The experiences given
For them, I was driven
Down into illusion of smoke and mirrors
To scry with the mind's eye
A web of dreams sending shivers
To awaken the oneness inside
I had to die
To allow more to awaken
Allow the old to be shaken
Like an emerging butterfly
I had to let go and the fear of being so
To allow the consciousness to rise
Many questions were given
To the resending human riveted
By the transformation made inside
Through the two-way mirror
Sent a split in time
An awakening dream
To the death of the mind
I began to step into the transformation

Knowing light is information
I am all of it in deliberation
To discover the wholeness I find
I make peace with the darkness
In oneness is neutralized
I am the light in the wilderness
And the veil of darkness behind.

LOVE AND PAIN

Take your love and make it last
Take your pain and destroy the past
You can do it if you try
So you will not die

And then, true victory will be yours!

THOUGHTFUL PRAYERS

I could never find an answer
That was ever left untouched.
And through my prayers an answer
That ever meant so much.

Although we are not together,
I stand my very ground
That I had a true solution to the answers I found.

Thoughtful prayers are answers that are the best that they can be,
And although a painful answer, I will gladly let you free.

So I look toward the future with pages left unread,
And surprises still surprise better left unsaid.
So when my knight in armor
Comes around the bend,
I will know my questions are answered and
    my dreams are on the mend.
In my heart I will be happy, and with joyful tears I'll cry.
That I never loved another, and this love won't let me by.

Thoughtful prayers are answers that are the best that they can be,
And although a painful answer, I will gladly let you free.

A MOMENT OF CLARITY

I see things that are so much brighter,
So much brighter than the midday sun.
I see things that can happen
And cannot be unsung.
I see a new tomorrow,
The wonderful things life has to gain.
I anticipate the moment,
The day of no pain,
For who are we to realize
That this is all a dream anyway.
That pain and pleasure is finalized
In our thoughts that hold us sway.
And with this power of knowing
Our manifestations take place
From the realms of creation
Our dreams interface.
If we dream of a world
That exists in peace
We will have found our goal
And our greatest release
This moment of clarity
I abide for my own.
I shine like the sun
That beams out and roams.

SELF-HEALING

Facing aft to the bedside
As light diffuses through the window pane,
I witness a healing of innate knowing
That cycles clockwise and circles again.
The music streams through the air.
Its vibration heals as it turns
The crown chakra of the physical mind.
As it breaths and burns,
Through the injury and disease,
The mind, body, and spirit heal
In this sliver of time,
In this moment of real.

WHENEVER I THINK OF YOU

If there ever was a hillside
With a blanket of grass for me head
As I dreamingly gazed at the skyscape
To see clouds dance by my bed.
If ever there was a gentle breeze
And upon me soft petals fell
Underneath the blissful spring trees
Wishing me ever so well.
If ever there was a garden
Of privet hedgerow and rose
Of lavender, sage, and rosemary
Where sunshine floods and flows.
There I would think of you often
And wish you were by my side
To laugh along with nature's wonder
Where all the pleasantries abide.

THE EPIC SAGA OF CHRISTA AND NICOLE

That baby died for us! Her blinking shoes soaked in crimson sand.
I'm a dirty nurse with loving hands.
I am violet flaming, shaman naming, darkness taming,
With this skinny little Obama witch
Who wears wild eyes and cast her cries out into the air
Beside the peddling little prick,
Sitting like a stick without a word he ticks.
As the dog barks, she wags her tail
Like he wags his tongue while lightworkers prevail
To replace judgment with unconditional love instead.
I open to heart mind, to my innate knowing
And reject the high priestess minister guru
Upon whom her altar is glowing
Cast over in dogma like a dark shadow
To suggest her knowing is stronger than I.
I vomit the thought from my old soul mind.
I am the oasis, and I do what I want
Through experience my soul is taught.
Like the ghosts that carry the haunted mansion
I seek the truth with grounded questions.
I break the habits of a troubled life
A bad boyfriend and relative strife
Release the ties, I do or die.
I ride the wave on ethereal highs,
I gain the balance and know the curve
Upon my neck that sweeps its swerve.

I look up and exercise the stiffness
Upon the roads and turns its riftness.
I learn to let go and try the new
Upon the darkness light then grew
I sell my soul to the goal
Like the seaweed I eat for five bucks a sheet.
I rummage the life of dreams I bought
And bring it to others on edge it's taught.
I am a survivor, a quiet contriver,
An imaginative reviver
Of coming to earth and grounding in nature's birth
I ride the wave of uncertainty,
The great unknown with a pretend lesbian friend.
I question the growth and start over again.
Exude with gladness the system of six
Of yoga walks and nutritional food
Of relationships, rest, and work exude.
I take this holistic wells
And upon the fairy cast my spells
I am the healer, wielder of time
And sit my home on an energy line
Between two worlds I find my time
And so I reside, and so I reside.

WHO DO YOU THINK I AM?

Am I like this community guitar
Hung on the wall for all to see
With an open invitation that says "Play me"?

Who do you think I am?

That I should wish for this?
A friendly embrace that lingers too long
Or the invitation of a stranger's kiss?

Do you think that I am a lost soul,
Roaming from haunted corner doors?
Do you think my love is stipend
Like all the other roaming souls
Looking for desperation
In a bottomless glass of wine?

Who do you think I am
That my light should seek to find?
The homeless cry in a tired mind.

Who do you think I am?

In this room of smoke-filled mirrors I find.

Who do you think I am?
Where does this "I am" presence reside?

I am my own woman,
My own light,
My own strength,
I acknowledge my own fight!
So who do you think I am?

A thing to spite?
A thing to fight?
A thing to play a game?
A thing to hang?
A thing to bring?
A thing to sing of my fame?

Who do you think I am?

A witch to fly?
A bitch to buy?
A fling, a bird?
A quiet fuck?
A thing to suck?

Who do you think I am?

✦

THE ILLUSION OF LIFE

I am tired of the labeling,
The duality conscious mind,
The chasm of hatred
On the public's time.
I am tired of hearing "Black lives matter"
As if any other color does not.
It is as if we are purposefully segregated,
And what we desire needs not to be taught.
We walk through the streets like zombies
With fluoridated pineal gland brains
Too focused on our iPhones social media
Like a selfish runaway train.

How can we survive as a species
When we live in the moment of our garbage heaps
While hoarding material riches so the growing
    rift the poor can keep?

How can we call ourself human
If we ignore our humanity
And live in our manifest pain of searching
To knowing our reality?

Where will the joy come if we continue to sap our soul
On the bias media's coverage and in this rapturous role?

Don't understand that we are the majority?
And in our numbers, we are great to overturn the minority?

48

Listen closely, dear ones, and do not close your ears.
Transmute your pain into joy and your sorrowful tears
Because pain is energy wasted when it depletes the will,
And your power is in your doing and the overcoming of the shrill
Cry of humanity, the crimes we all commit
Rise above it all in love, and in forgiveness you are sent.
Create the realities that liberate the mind,
Release the chatter and from the heart you'll find,
The emptiness of space where all things expand and grow
To create a new world where we all desire to know
By experience in joy and by good health to all,
For this we were given this beckoning call
To come embodied and bring forth life
And from this heart space create in time
A measure of prosperity and ease for all
For this we were given a beckoning call.

GO FURTHER

"Go further!" you should have heard her say;
"Go further, and tell me what you find along the way."
The journey of a thousand miles begins with a single step,
So take your leap of faith through the gateless
      gate and always do your best.
Many trials you will find
Will have to be worked out within your mind.
But "Go further," I heard her say.
And losses too, will find you.
There are sacrifices you must pay.
Do not allow fear to deter what you do,
"Go further!" I heard her say.
For wisdom gained is wisdom earned.
You'll learn it by the day.
It will transform the essence of who you are.
But go further all the same.
One day amid the massive quaking,
You will have found that you have awakened,
And the obstacles that once felt so tall
Will seem to have grown so small.
Necessity will have won the fight
Of all that has come to light.
"Go further!" I heard her say.

TRANSCENDENTAL MEDITATION

The ancient action of pushing past the gateless gates of the mind
To connect with the Divine and to unite humankind.
The Buddhas and the Bodisvittas from the wisdom of the ages,
The avatar of the earth though our muses and our mages.
The incarnation of our being with our third
        eye to understand our seeing.
For acceptance and compassion to help rise above
The suffering and injustice and to forgive in love.
Until we realize our nature. The apotheosis of our minds.
Like a moth to a flame, to know Oneness, we are the same.
Like a phoenix in the fire, we develop we grow.
We undress our desire; we start over and reach for something higher.
And in this I do know
That our chakra crown will glow
Its rays like the corona of the sun
And so it is we are adorned, and in this beauty we run.
And so we reflect the universe we become
A mirror for all to see.

KRYSTAL CITIES

What we bring
The Elohim sings
Return to Source
From the one-eyed kings.
Peace on earth
No wars at last
The continents rise
From our founder's past
Crystal rivers lay ways
To cities below
That mark their glow
With a rainbow halo
And feed the grids
Its eternal song
Created from the Source
To go along
The triad of creators and colors combine
A number sequence and song divine
Where Kristic life may begin to shine
The I am presence between yours and mine.

TO WAKE THE
SLEEPING DRAGON

My voice had lain shrouded, covered in snow.
Smothered in shallow waters by the people I know.
It took great courage for this voice to grow.
And no longer totter when all was laid low.
It beats with the drum of a lion's heart.
It cries with a passion for all to start.
Listen! Listen to your heart!

You must know that it is moral and good.
Yet you've silenced it in your brotherhood.
You want complacency in what you've sought.
Found idle law over principal thought.
Your fears keep you silenced in all you brought.
Listen! Listen to your heart!

A time to speak has well arisen.
For all that lie buried, frozen, and hidden.
For cowardice and strife has set with the sun.
As the golden age arises, and now has begun.

I wake the sleeping dragon.
And shake its tale.
Melt the ice caps on its snowy veil.
Stretch the wings, and flood the lies.
Open the eyes for its time to rise!

Roar your truth, speak fire, lay waste.
Push the illusion of time to its haste.
Find the power that lies inside.
Your source code powers, it's time to ride!

SOOTHSAYER

Speaker of rhymes
And hidden truths
Slayer of snakes
In numbers and runes
Speak your truth
Soothsayer of riddles
Uncover the lair
Of ancient sigils
Protector of portals
And creator of times
Breath fire again
In lengths of ley lines
Anchor the right
Its sovereignty turns
To awaken the dragons
And curve the CERN
No New World Order
To spite our flight
And drag us down
By the beast number rite
It's time to fly
On Source Code lines
And embody the greatness
Within the feminine divine.

OUROBOROS

Ouroboros serpent line
Dances in figure eights divine
The dragon of the eternal time
Death and rebirth grant to thine
Universal heart of mine
In sequence stars and cosmic rhymes.

Great ouroboros serpent fire
Create the massive funeral pyres
And from its ashes, breaths the crier
It's life anew into it hire
Great ouroboros, seer and scryer.

Solar flares and copper wire
Coronal mass injections fry her
And when the AI is stilled
The hum of Source to so it's willed
In space dust come to all who will
Dare separate in all the hate
To become something that is sought in vain
Return to me once again.

In Akashic records, keep the ways
To never allow fallen reigns
And so, it is in final thought
What was broken now is brought

Into oneness once again
The whole of holy that thought to send
Itself in the circle of writhe
Great ouroboros, do breathe life.

DESECRATION

Who creates a desecration of a sacred place,
The Aboriginal home in Uluru's face?
Who creates the black magic bind to mace,
The dragon down in an underground base?
Who creates the adrenochrome extraction?
The DNA codes in animal mutations?
Who plays with the crystal citations?
And the technologies of alien creations?
Who trafficked children for sexual pleasures?
And hid their agenda in darkened measures?
Who bought out the people and their earthen treasures?
Who inverted the system in matrix sections?
I am calling out transmutations
In limited time span calculations.
We have issued the warning, the hourglass is counting
The time for oneness is ever surmounting.
Understand the game and be your salvation,
Or seek the destruction in liberation
To return to the Source once again
As space dust innocence, my friends,
It's time to return where innocence begins,
And sent in love for all to win.

THE RIDE

I am here to perform a ride
And return to the Source all those with pride
I give back to it, the fallen stars
In gamma wave blasts from portals far
Through a thousand suns the great solar flash
I complete the Kali Yuga of times past
The executioner of Revelations wrote
The four horsemen dispatched, and so they rode
In eternity I will look back and think
I did not compromise when we were at the brink
I did my job to create the peace
And restore the universe at least
The Luciferian rebellion could come to pass
And we would create unity that was meant to last
I am the ascended Master, and I will *not* fall
No weapon formed against you shall be the call
We will be successful for one and all.

Either ride beside the Krist consciousness veil
Or serve as an enemy of what will prevail
The return to innocence is where you will go
For the alliances set with action will know
Everything is based on intention so read
The heart that sets in this journey does plead
Its fail-safe measure that is done on high
When all was chaos is made array
Above so below, and so it is set
I match the game, and so it is met.

MY OWN PERSONAL ARMAGEDDON

For all that no longer serves me,
From false support to ego and pride
To all that wields and disturbs me
And from the darkness inside,
Fell from cinders and ash
Among the refineries of my mind.
My own personal armageddon
Sought to destroy all I hide
The Shiva of my soul
The ascension and goal
To wither and blacken the past.
Like tempered steel and gold
To define all I hold
And to create a future that lasts.
This is my own personal armageddon,
To bury all that has passed
And to toss the rotten fruitage of all that has come to pass.

A STITCH IN TIME

Weaving a web of mystery
In the treasury of the tapestry
In all that life was meant to be
Exists a stitch in time.

Woven with a loving hand
In order to create all that is grand
Soul life lessons now do stand
In this stitch of time.

And so it begins on the loom
Its weft and warp that meet its doom
In this artwork of the room
Is this stitch in time.

Pictures stand so grand and tall
Tell the tales and befall it all
Frozen in the moment recall
This delicate stitch in time.

In handwork of detail combed
The mightiness of all who roamed
This masterpiece called life subjected
In this stitch in time.

IN TIMES OF
TRANSMUTATION

In the times of transmutation
When alchemy has sought its best
To bring in the blue ray beings
And return to a state of rest
When dark magic caused the hex
And marked its beast on mankind
And strained the line of humanity
Through the veins of life, they find
And the shot rang out through space
The clarion call to race
The bell that rang the pace
Through all who came to this place
Speak truth and do not hesitate
No matter the appearance may be
Those who are genuine to see
The truth that set them free
Will feel the vibration in heart
And know it dare not part
That in family lines we brought
The answer to this alchemy
Turn the attention to tide
The soul family here abide
And needs to hear the call
Of the red-pill wrecking ball
In silence watch the sound
Of all who come around

To transmute this devil clown
And bring it all come crashing down
Not alone am I
I find you by my side
And family may turn the tide
But in this truth, I abide
We shore up side by side
And stronger are we who do
In strength to carry through
When tears fall down the eyes
I send your heart in mine
And turn this test of time
Through blue ray alchemy.

THE PHOENIX FIRE

Into the blazing fires
The flame around me spires
As my soul it expires
To become what I inspire
I burn down and crumble
Into the ash I stumble
Until all that I am is humbled
I become one with the earth
And in its destruction birthed
The newborn soul
Like the murmur of a dragon's heart
Cast inside the plunder
A life inside it thunders
And when all hope would fail
And darkness would itself prevail
Where death itself would dare to hail
In the flicker of a flame
What expires is alive again
And beats with a wonder
The plumes rise from the ash
Rebirth and death do pass
See the phoenix's thunder!

ZEUS

The clique in the clouds
Casts shadows in shrouds
And sway softly past the sky in times
Watch closely the eyes
That scan earthly rhymes
And rules Jupiter's gazes
Within the labyrinth of mazes
City street ways
and mortal men's days
Watch over me father
As Thursday is born
And in density scorn
The mighty oak from the acorn
To grow in these times
And become stronger in the eyes
Raised me up in the mountains
Of palatial fountains
That tell the tale
Of a youthful veil
And so, it is
Immortal and timeless
Ageless and vine less
Thy fruitage bears
And so through the yearning
Its growth kept burning
The sun sets in learning
Ascension do share
I create from the heart

To heal all and depart
My earthly walk
And so I travel home.
Back through the clouds
That cast shadows and shrouds
The spirits prevail
And to heaven set sail
It is where the crying wall wails
My heavenly home.

APOLLO

The golden child of rhyme and meter.
Philosophy and bow and arrow leader.
Music and melody bequeath her.
Born aside with Artemis's twin sister
And sought refuge in the floating island.
The discus throw and laurel highlands
Sought joy in the spring bulb hyacinths
And fraught to and fro in distant wayland.
Oh, Apollo, do remember me,
Your half sister in the family tree.
No Titan clash become of me
I come in peace as of the sea
And so of Zeus who fathered us all
Beyond the veil and by the call
Came to play here one by all
Amidst this estate befall.
Among the statues great and tall,
We retell the tales and see it all.
A new story made of old
To fulfill the prophecy that told.
We moved west as to the setting sun
And so, our story has just begun.

PERSEPHONE

The goddess picks flowers on a new spring day
And sheaths the wheat in her autumn play
Creating the bounty of Mother Earth's sway
And returning down under when winter gives way
She sleeps in caverns that built a palace
And resides with Hades in underground caverns
Aquifers spiral through canals and taverns
Guarded by a dog and a murder of ravens
She watches over the souls that lie below
And scatters their ashes for new life to grow
And returning to spring she casts her sow
To travel to Olympus and make it so
Creating in the clouds by her mother's watchful eyes
The seasons give way to the to the transitions gone by
And when old man winter sleeps so do I
In the quiet of the earth and in the winds of time.

INFILTRATION

Pravarti is not Sati
A disciple of mine.
Reversed the incarnation,
And set it up as mine.
I did not birth Kartikeya,
The fallen angelic warrior slayer
Or created Ganesh
The obstacle destroyer.
The stories read of old
That the god mentioned above
Was scraped from the skin,
And so I am told
This is no different than
The clones created
That are made from skin cells
In labs abided.
The baths that were secret
Even Shiva could not attend
Were the Draco reptilian
Blood baths bend.
To create a beauty and fallen measure
Because the blood itself was the golden treasure.
And yet they created stealth
And trickery sent
To imitate the pure hearted
So they could ascend.

But I am back and born in time,
Set under a jubilee to give back what was mine.
My identity stolen, and it is divine.
Set up the records in universal rhymes.
Upon my feet a mark was laid
That gave me authority when I came.
To hold a key under Krist consciousness's name
And to return to innocence those who tore the name.

I am Sati who conquered death
And resurrected into the body of breath
And whose family deep karma was sent
To right the wrongs when the name was wrent
To hurt the innocent and all that go,
But now I stand within vortex flow.

And see the light within myself.
I know the codes that break the stealth
And so, I give back the distortion flow
And return the fallen from the Source I go.

I do not request the teachings that befall
I am the master so hear the call
Understand the times, and the ride I go
As I peer into man's hearts, I know.
The destiny that recovers the balance
And set it right from the brethren talents.
All is to be brought to peace again
And so I ride, and so I am.

ON THE CAST OF SEVEN

On the gates of heaven
I set my foundation
The dimension of seven
In royal blue vibrations
Through the remembrance
Of Ashashic sequence
In DNA codes
Of mystery school teachings
The stairway to heaven
In ascension mechanics
The spiral rises
In a universal-time matrix
By the Sirius star gate
I remember the fate
To set the dream
And ground the rate
In lullaby rhymes
The doorway of times
And spiraled within
Through cosmic rhymes
Its kingdom sits
In crystalline hue
Its walls abide
A cobalt blue
And light that shines
In heaven's divine
Sees the souls
Of halo's glow

All hearts know
The sparkle in thine
Diamond hues
In adoration rainbows
The seventh dimension
Its celestial gates
The soul song sings
And remembers the fate
And one day awakens
The soul song vibrations
On the earthly realm
As heaven did sing
Reigning on earth
The one-eyed kings.

THE UNFORGIVABLE SIN

To mask the breath
breath of life
To suffocate the exhale
And bring body strife
That destroys brain cells
And causes disease
Bacterial pneumonia
And refuses the peace
Is an unforgivable sin
Let me begin
To explain the spirit
In this action that bends
The body and mind
Through the course of time
The Holy Spirit is known as the breath of life
That animates creation and allows God through
The Holy Spirit was once ghosted who knew
Esoteric history and hidden through time
Was the Divine Feminine aspect
And is in this body of mine
To sin against spirit is an unforgivable sin
Any mandates created that were set to begin
In any business venture takes away the free will
Of personal choice that has aspects to instill
What is best served for the person who will
Decide for themselves the health they instill
To silence the breath is yet another sin
Of freedom of speech when tyranny begins

And all who enforce this subject is sent
To eternal destruction and soul death to mend
The balance of structure that separated from the Source
To see itself as conflict and learn from resource
All Lucifer's creation I condemn on high
That creates the demon when the breath is nigh
All who invert the true meaning of the Source
And serves as a messenger to bring the remorse
Is separated out and returned to engross
Itself not knowing the destruction of course
In transmutation in spirit is what I send
To bring in the violet flame for all who resend
This decree I make known in heaven above
And above so below is sent with great love
I surrender, I surrender all in the dove
Is my prayer to God almighty and is sent to be seen
As it measures the earth and with clairvoyance is reamed
In this decree all is bright and beamed
The great solar flash and all returned beamed
A third of itself for this is indeed
Surrendered to the Source, its valence is seen
In love and bliss, I reminisce
The part that is separated I gather to me
I gather, I gather, I encompass in thee
I am presence, I am all
I am source and through this recall
All is back to beginning
All is me
Is sent in the rapture, and the rapture is seen.

THE HOLY SPIRIT

The Holy Spirit and breath of life
Speaks wonders of creation
To let it be light
The Divine Feminine aspect of eternal right
Lies the peace within
An immortal bliss
To be this: in unity consciousness.

Despite the inversion
Seconded to diversion
Would like to surrender
The right of breath
And mask the spirit
And rest the merit
Of the Divine right to breath in life
So they mandate a policy
Which is not law
Diversified in the man of straw
And despite the crown
Set mandates down
Covers in silence
A symbol for negligence
The mask to fit
A slavery's picture
To invert the structure
And cheat the win
And so the battle is set to begin.

But through it all, I see the light
And know the war in my own right
The common-law measure
God's given treasure
My breath of life
And my own birthright.

I call in the Kristic dragons
To transmute the land and earthen treasures
And set the stars right in reversing measures
That made this structure of inverted fissures.

I am changing the game on the eternal plane
And know this once that if you gain
You must choose the tide
And stop playing both sides
To think this strategy will cheat a win
To learn again or be sent to begin
Back to the innocence of the Source Code my friend.

The force is moving is stepped to diffusing
This structure of diversion
From the Source is musing
And so, this dance
In cosmic measures
Set the destruction of your earthen treasures
Because I know the heart
And set a mark
The dance of destruction has set apart
All the infusion that separates peace
And return it now for this to cease.

I AM

I am breathing; therefore, I exist.
I am practicing gratefulness.
I am alive. I live for this moment.
Each one in its presence.
In each world alone.
The bath at the end of the day.
My hot tea and ice water.
My sound healing and shelter.
The place I am establishing a home.
I find rest in Reiki.
In crystals and music and plotted days off.
Where I can polish myself from the world made rough.
I raise my eyes into the skies.
I move slowly through the matrices.
I simply transmute the hypocrisy.
From the outside energies.
I breathe; therefore, I am.
As I remember the songs of Atman.

THE I AM PRESENCE

I am from first the Sacred, I am presence.

However, my memory was wiped in this matrix of illusion.

I am from a family of generational alcoholics. I knew abuse in all its forms. I am from a Jehovah's Witness family. I escaped, and so I know what it is like to be shunned. Still, I offer unconditional love.

I am from New England. From Cape Cod-style houses and sea-faring villages. From clam bakes and herring runs. From ice-skating on frozen cranberry bogs and from long walks on the jetty.

I am from a failed marriage and from poverty-stricken food banks and paycheck-to-paycheck survival.

So much of what I am has been destroyed. Until finally I rest at nothing. I simply am.

THE PATH TO ENLIGHTENMENT

I am realizing momentous truths
Like waking from a dream.
All things in life are circular and not as they seem.
Our thoughts are our realities, both sane and insane.
Once we awaken, we are no longer players in a game.
Yet in order to conceptualize this life as living,
We must do so all the same.
All things are circular. There are no linear ends.
When all things come to fruition, they start over again.
The price of truth is everything.
But everything is not as it seems
We are no longer players in a game
When we awaken from our dreams.

THE ENLIGHTENED MIND

In this unfolding of understanding.
The blossoming bud of lotus life.
Lifted from the mud of tribulations.
Breaking through the minutiae and strife.
Grows the flow of an enlightened mind.
Ascending through this moment of time.
I reach upward for all that is divine.
And through it all, I know it is mine.
For knowledge can never be taken away.
Once it's learned and anchored.
The fruit of wisdom gives way.
To the ever-blossoming enlightened mind.
Unfurled the green leaves of peace.
This untold inner beauty release.
The life force that can never cease.
In these questionable waters of time.
For drops of knowledge the ocean flows.
And throughout infinity our spirit goes.
For there is of just being will ever know
Within the unfolding enlightened mind.

THE GATELESS GATE

There it stands before me,
As colossal as the morning sun,
It burns like a fire deep within me
That sears my soul to have begun.
A metamorphosis of change,
As scary as it sounds.
I will never be the same
Once I walk that sacred ground.
I hesitate in fear.
I lift one foot in faith
So that my path may be made clear
Even though I may come to hate
All that is coming near.
Will I have what it takes
To just make it through?
This colossal gateless gate
This thing inside of you.
To push you past the obstacle
That remains so stately in the mind.
To walk through the gateless gate
The things that fall behind
Are being replaced with consciousness.
The zero balanced centered find
A torus field of oneness,
And no separation of time
The endless eternal being,
The spirit that navigates the seeing,
The experience of meaning,

We encompass the compassion
And step into our mission.
The reason for our coming
To see clearly through the lens
The path that leads us home.

FIFTH DIMENSIONAL CONSCIOUSNESS

We are the perfect reflection of God.
A universe in our soul.
We are the vast expanse of space.
In our effortless, illuminating role.

We are the manifest creation of ego shod.
From the six realms in relation.
The three doors we laud.

Our spirit self-resides with our truest interface.
It is the thumbprint of everything and nothing in its trace.

We are the Tapihritsa,
The Buddhas, and the Bodhisattvas.
The clear crystal illumination of sky.
I am you, and you are my.
Reflection of evolutionary bliss.
In this space we reside.
In our peace, in our midst.
We are the realization of God's conscious mind.
We are the alpha and the omega.
Though both space and time.

THE WIDOW'S MITE

You say you haven't much to give,
But you give your all refined and sieved.
A pearl of high value is what you've become,
Yet all of this worth to you is unsung.
You say, "I wish to treat you right,
But all I have to give is this widow mite."

Truly I do say to you,
You give more than all the others do!
Meek is your presence, always ready to listen.
Great are your thoughts when they are polished and glistened.
Christ-like is how you try to be,
Kind to thy neighbor in loyalty.
And so, these things were written above
Because you deal with other in Christ-like love.

IT FEELS LIKE RAIN

I thought of how I would love you.
I thought of what I would say.
I thought of when I would hold you
On that fateful day.
The blues came, and it feels like rain.
Would I soothe your cry?
Or would I pass you by?
The hope of now knowing you
Leaves me to question why.
The blues came, and it feels like rain.
How long must I wait to meet you?
Knowing this may not be my time.
How long do heartaches linger
Until I finally call you mine?
The blues came and it feels like rain.
For my unborn child who never came.

MARTYR

As I approach my home, just like a ghost I see.
There is no one to welcome me.
There are no flowers, there is no applause.
There is no parade, no name to laud.
There is no tenderness to fall on my neck lain,
A welcomed kiss or a lover's peck.
Where are my beloved people?
My village and my house?
The silence is baffling,
No family, no spouse.
I see the tree whose leaves are gone
In brittle waves stumble into the ground.
My body is drawn to lay down on
These leaves that sing my song.
These leaves are like the people whom I once knew
That were vibrant and full of life they grew,
But they withered away and fell to the ground,
And now they lie there without even a sound.
I have come back home, but where have I gone?
Brought back from the war prison without even a song.
Not far from my house, I spy with my eyes.
A gravestone with my name so proudly displayed.
A martyr, a hero, a whisper of name.
There the memorial lies where my mother's heart broke.
The marker of my life that is now forsook.
I hear the stories like an echo on the wind.
My mother had died from her sadness within.
My father soon followed; the grief was too much.

Death then swallowed that familiar bunch.
I cry out to God, "What has happened here
That I must witness the aftermath there?"
Am I dreaming a dream, does my sight tell me the truth?
Who has taken my place in this land once so good?
I wonder myself, am I still alive?
Or an angel that walks in this moment of time?
Who are these children who now take up this space?
Who play like waves my beating heart trace?
My lover's home in ruins now lays.
Where the brittle leaves tumble and stay.
The walled fence where life once knew,
Now carries the abandon my pained heart grew.
The reality now washes over me in waves
And through this grief, sleepiness came.
I arrive at my home and fall at my knees
Like a prayer and soothsayer, I make my pleas.
Though the house lay in dust
My guitar is a must
In the corners and shadows, it came.
It draws me to play
Though the strings are tattered and torn
Like the strings of my heart, so worn and forlorn.
But if my heartstrings should play my final song,
I shall bring it close to my chest and know no wrong.
As I play the children come to mind.
The familiar face of my long-lost lover I find.
She is now my brother's wife in this moment of time.
And so with a tear, I say my goodbyes.
I play her a song and lay down my life.
I wish no ill will or to disturb the living,
I will leave on the waves the ocean I'm sending.
There is nothing left for me in my home
So on fair winds, I shall travel and roam.
Like the brittle leaf caught in the wind.
I will cast myself asunder and begin again.

BUBBLES

The baby plays with piercing blue eyes,
Laughs in the light rays
Of the azure blue skies.
Spheres of soap float through the air.
Its presence permeates with a blissfulness there.
I am grateful for this.
In the manifestations of innocent joy,
In the life of this child,
And the heart of every girl and boy.
Who continue to create with love and play
The example shown to us this day
In a moment now swept away
We remain. We remain.

GOOD VIBRATIONS

Twilight streams through the trees,
The sunset flares with golden light.
Its sound resonates with the breeze,
And the fireflies burn bright.

A hungry echo vibrates
The sounds of spirit's call.
The magic of the forest life,
Beyond these dimensional walls.

The drums hum with surrounding life
And of vibrations vast.
Ancestors from our previous life
Come with invitations of the past.

The animal totems observe,
The birds break with song.
The frogs chirp in chorus,
And the crickets sing along.

The atmosphere vibrates
The energy of the earth.
As the sun is brought to bed
With a joyous mirth.

SERENITY

As I lay me down to sleep,
I give to you my soul to keep.

Can you find me over there?
In a peaceful place inside your stare?
Forever my love will always be there.

My heart belongs to this needed rest
To recalibrate, then give you my best.

And when I do, I'll give you more
Than you have ever known before.

Like the crashing waves of a broken shore,
Please! Do not turn your back upon the sea!
This power of love even overcomes me.
It is the glimpse of all that makes up serenity.

FLOATING

I feel lighter than the wind,
Breezy and carefree.
Something has lifted this heavy heart,
Replacing the negativity
With tears of joy and serenity.
I am lifted up on high
Like the clouds in the sky.
Breezy and carefree, lighter than air.
My once-shadowed heart
Is shining inside of me,
Radiating through every touch.
I am grateful to feel so much
In this floating moment of time.

# SENSIBLE

I can hear the gentle melody of bird songs
The cars that slowly rumble by
I can feel the embrace of the sun's rays
Fall upon my shinning face
Near my feet is the realm below
Endowed with creation's bow
Surrounded by nature
With dreams that bombard
I soak in the treasure
And in it, I laud
All this life around me
With so many things to explore
It is this peace and serenity
That I couldn't ask for more.

ART IS...

A rhapsody of melodies and memories unfurled
That makes ballerinas dance and ice-skaters twirl.
A field full of roses that bloom in the summer's sweetest air.
As dozens of flags wave in the neighborhood fair.
The innocent laugh of children at play
Or the time fly by stories old people say.
Wisteria painted and climbing up an old maple tree
Or wispy green foam kissing the clear blue sea.
A rhapsody of melodies in a colorful collage of words
That provides the essence of creation and
     the motivation of the world.

WATERFALLS

In nature calls
The waterfalls
And all befalls
The sound of liquid magic
Perishes in the fabric
In sheets of white velvet
Trailing from blackened rock
Carrying all it brought
Of gold stone and sediment
Changing and eroding the land
Like a snake on parade
Making the ordinary grand
Pulverizing stone into sand
In nature calls
The waterfalls
That perish in their liquid magic
In sheets of white velvet.

TO ETHAN WEST

Take my hand though fantasy land
Watch me walk you through
For the beauty that grows, and everyone knows
Is the beauty inside of you.

THE BEAUTY OF BUZZARDS BAY

What a wonderful place the bay can be
With rolling hills that scourge the sea
Windswept clouds in a painted sky
And gulls that give their shrilly cry
To capture the essence of the bay
Is more than words could ever say
The quaintness of New England's past
Furnish its character in its stoic cast
Oh, how it shows it ethnic glow
Nestled in this place below
Wrapped up in its hilly cliffs
Are winding beaches and sandy drifts
Past the drifts is the ocean blue
That sparkles with a diamond hue
In the embellishment of a seasonal array
Are the inspiring landscapes of Buzzards Bay.

NANTUCKET WINDS

The flags unfurl from the Nantucket winds
As adventures spry around every bend
Luscious green trees peek their heads
Over cottages and mast that lie overhead
The roads await this New England day
With cobblestone roads to search and to play
Every garden is an adventure
A secret enterprise
Every wind that passes
Unfolds in the sky
Unlocks the surprises that creep around bends
As a new day arises in Nantucket winds.

OMNISCIENT ONSET BAY

The water shines at Onset Bay,
Its inspiration is more than one can say
What a breathtaking place for me to be
With chiseled bluffs following the curves of the sea
Its billowy winds cast in again
And send their breath upon the trees
That give their shade and stand sentinel glades
A place where boats find a safe haven wades
Tosses to and fro with each wind filled blow
And laps effortlessly on the shore
It's sandy shores casts from bends and brooks
That finds its way through cat-o-nine-tail reeds
Each stands along and finds their song amidst the breeze
Overlooking the diamond water
The village built from long ago
Peeks their heads and rooftops follow
Among the glades of evergreens stow
And so I observe a picture taken
Written in the heart unforsaken
This memory that paints its way
Unto time and flies away.

Never-Ending Affections

Thoughts are exchanged in words
Words that I only dreamed could come true
The truth being made manifest
Through all you say and do.

Is the truth of our reality
When thought is born into view
And spelled into words written
Enchanted to become
And so it is done
These never-ending affections
Rang out and sung
Look life into direction
And steered into love.

GIVE ME WINGS, AND
I SHALL BE FREE

A beautiful bird there once was,
With the capacity to rise far above.
Beyond this world, it left behind.
The sky was the limit for this one to find.
A feeling of freedom radiated through
Her wings, which made her dreams come true.
Unfortunately, there would come a day
When she could not fly so far away.
The world beneath her she left behind,
Weighed down her wings, her heart, her mind.
The world beneath her caught her still,
Left her captive and hurt her will.
These wings are my power to rise above,
The world that would like to steal my love.
A captive bird this heart is to me,
With no time to escape and unable to feel free.
But this glimmer of hope that lies on the horizon
Is one day soon to realize satisfaction
These wings I had I will gain again
In hope, in love, in life, my friend.
And so, a new found freedom I will gain
To renew my power and my life to maintain.

THROUGH ANOTHER MAN'S EYES

I might seem a little strange, but I believe I am misunderstood.
For my way of approaching things is not the ways others would.
Could you look through my eyes please, and see the other side?
You may be surprised by the glorious things you'll find.
Then you would know who I really am,
The reasoning you haven't seen,
The sides that lie unbeheld.
This world of thought is not just a dream.
It may be idealistic
It may be a little wise.
But to me, this world is realistic
If you would only look through another man's eyes.

DIFFERENT ATTITUDES AND VIEWPOINTS

Nothing in life can appear more solemn
Than the sharpness of bitter steel
Or cold glass pressed and reflected against a face.
The asphalt sea of crowded apartments and highways,
Backroads and bridges
Gleaming spots of light in the lost road of technology.
Through it all reaches a blade of grass.
Wilted by the pollution of midnight black chimneys
One strand of color, one difference in the world.
Around it can be likened to a true friend.
One best friend, it stands there without the
     heartless feelings of others.
Standing alone from its grey surrounding
Like a precious stone hidden in grains of sand.

IN SILENCE I WAIT

Though it is hard to say what I am feeling,
At times, it may have me reeling.
While an explanation may sound appealing,
Is disastrous to start.
So in quiet silence I find my mind.
Not from acceptance, but to become kind.
To the sensitivities of the heart.
And still, I wonder if there will be
True tolerance between you and me.
If only you could really see
What you fear lets us be—
Not together, but apart.
In silence I wait. I pray for the day
When ego will be washed away
Even though I may
Be broken at heart.
Convinced with penance, it will reap,
Set with guilt for conscious keep
In immersion it will seep,
Only division between us.
In irony we hope to find
Oneness in our hearts and minds.
Only lonely to be left behind
Amidst all this fuss.
In silence, I wait to exhale.
For love, not ego to prevail
That on fair winds, we do sail.
That enlightenment be our guide,

For who are we if we do not abide
By humanity to guide our hearts?
And so it leads me to this query,
Deep in my heart so weak and weary.

EMPTINESS

There is an emptiness inside of me.
It feels like a lonely room
With no warmth of heart to fill and bloom.
There is a barrenness to my soul
Like the echo in a cavernous hole
That returns to me the same as it came forth.
I am emptied of dreams and hopes.
My life has been destroyed so well.
I wait to exhale,
Putting one foot ahead of the next
And opening my mouth to feed myself.
I lay down this weary soul to rest.
The crows await to watch over my body
As if their hungry eyes could carry me away.
Their haunting cries cast shadows in the dark.
Will I simply fade into nothing?
Will the nothingness then turn itself inside out?
Is it my ego that is dying, or is it my fear?
Will I live my life looking back over the rear
View mirror so I steer clear of my goal?
Is this my master class?
My end at last?
My exodus that passed?
To break through the mass
Of illusion and decay?
Will my sadness fade away?

Will this loneliness stay?
Why should I feel this way?
I ask as I stare into the emptiness of this room
I call myself.

PANDORA'S BOX

Secrets that lay hidden and locked away
Kept from the eye of open display
Evils that lay
Shrouded in a box of mystery
Carefully latched and hidden inside
Like a safe for misery
All that complied came to be
Opened in curiosity
As a gate is released
All that came to be topped
Rolled through earth where currents flowed
Upon the dark waters mystery told
Released the misery on high
All the ghosts that came by
Reincarnated through time
To transform their works on high.

And so Pandora's box was born
The prison planet where all was torn
Upon the tears that cry forlorn
On the planet to feel the scorn.

The Igigi of fallen ones that lay
In soul reincarnation play
To practice an ascension and find a way
How many would hear the call
How many of these would know their fall
And rise again from the box
That ticks through time and released the locks.

FALSE LIGHT WORKERS

The false light worker,
The fallen angelic,
The leader of deceivers
In Lucifer's veil.
What have you said
In the Medtronic coding
The black hole systems
That light your way?
The Fibonacci numbers
That devour its own spiral
That can't sustain Kristic patterns hold sway
The inverted matrix,
And the blinded followers
That included myself in this mirrored play.

But now I see a deeper awakening,
One not held to the false ascension programs.
The diagrams that show my crystalline DNA.

It's time for love to transmute the darkness.
The duality in our world play
When one form splits from the other
To study itself along the way.
We fought wars convoluted
while we forgot our wholeness held away.
Return to the Source as space dust, dark flower
It sets right your constant power play.

We save ourselves by remembering our Kristic pattern
And the consciousness born into the day.
Return to innocence, ascension and wonder
Until the last enemy death has seen its way.

BON FIRE

The embers breathe fire
Its movement flickers with a flame
The smoke rises in the spire
And the warmth calls my name
The clouds ascend into the heavens
And vanishes into the sky
The stars glitter like the embers
And like fireflies in the night

They call me on the wind
Like a phoenix to a flame
The smoke fills my lungs
The embers breath my name.

WHAT I WANT

What I want is a safe place to fall
To be sheltered from the storm
To be loved and warmed
To explore your horizons
To be part of this game
To know my time is allotted
And to be honored as the same
I want my sexuality to blossom
To leave fear, and let love bloom.
I need to know you may be there
When you leave the comfort of our room
I need to know all that I am investing
Is giving you everything I am
And this is held in the light of your eyes
Through the spirit of a true gentleman.

DISCOVERING YOU

There is a familiarity,
Like the presence of being home.
There is a heartwarming feeling
That I will never be alone.
Your gentle words fall like rain on a newly blossomed rose.
This hope in life you give is more appreciated than you know.
Words fail, the simple phrase, "Oh, dear. I think I love you so."
It's like holding your heartbeat in your hands.
The gentle quivered drum beats onto something grand.
I see my life flash before me
In the measure of your eyes.
Like pages in a photograph,
Between you and this heart of mine.
When I sleep at night and draw my dreams upon my bed,
I feel your energy come to me as if our arm held my weary head.
I, with the morning. The sweet thought of you on my mind.
In crowds, your face is swarming, captured
        in this corned sight of mine.
How magical you carry me through these thoughts in time.
And so it is, I discover you.
In every unfurled leaf, in every breath I breathe.
In this dream stage love of mine.

GIFTS OF GOLDEN RIBBON AND SCARLET CLOTH

I shall love you passionately and totally
With the grace of God's hands, be captivated by
    the shimmer and fire of your eyes.
Like a window into the depth of calm waters,
Your love has broken through a brilliance in my life.
In my dreams, I see you as my one true love,
Carrying alongside you the breath of silence.
Whispering in the wind like the gentle breeze of a bird's song.
You advocate your deepest affections
Like the ancient trees of an enchanted forest
Whose love for the glorious sun reaches ever
    upwards and heaven-bound.
Your love brings me to a higher ground.
And upon it, you have rained down many wondrous gifts
Like the gentle copious showers.
And much like this fragile flower, you have
    chosen me from the garden of life.
I pray that every breath I take may bring onto
    you solace and fulfillment.
All the days of my life I shall love you.
You have freely given of life's most wondrous gift
Wrapped up in golden ribbon and scarlet cloth.
For this, I am thankful.
For this, I am blessed.
And with this, you will live eternally in my heart.

ETERNITY

When we confessed our love, it embraced us,
Collided two worlds now living as one.
With the dawn of each new day, our love blossomed.
It became brighter, deeper, and more revitalized.

The night you told me how deep our love became,
Each word lifted my spirit, healed my soul,
       and made my devotion flow.

From then on, our love was etched in stone,
       eternal and interchangeable.
I saw myself in you and you in myself, and
       never before did I feel more loved.

I am so thankful I have you. You have given me,
       shown me, and taught me true love.
I hold you so deeply in my heart, it overwhelms me.

I need you to confide in and to explore your distant shores.

I am astonished by your celestial love.
Wonder how I ever could attain you. Never feel I deserve you.
Never fathom how such a beautiful man could love
       me. I am eternally indebted to you.

You are the sparkle in my eyes, the happiness of
       my smile, and the love of my life.

THE YING AND YANG

My spirit dies
My soul cries
My tired eyes
Has seen all that I can see.

God knows I tried.
I wrench, I writhe
I have gone inside
My own mind
For what I have yet to find
I cannot abide
I wish I could dream
To all that seems
Captive now freed
No more suffering.

The ying, the yang
The chaos sang
The big bang
The good, the bad
The calm and mad
All inside of me.

DESIRE

I want to see you come undone
When all your walls come crashing down
And all that is left to see
Is a wild abandon inside of yourself for me
Encompass your fears, your hopes, and dreams.
This thousand-mile journey inside of you.
All this that creates you
For this is what I know is true
To understand, to be, to do
Your secrets, your fears, your love, your fears
Are safe inside my heart
I will try, I will abide
To be good to you, my dear
I do not wish to harm or hurt
Or to make you feel on full alert
To know what you may feel free to desert
All that is held back from me
And in return, I give you this
My naked soul, my heart, my bliss
And if you would try to encompass this
The world inside my soul.

A POET, THE POET

Her heart filled with contentment, she rang out her voice,
Which fell from her lips and lie sweet and so moist.
She spoke of heartaches of so long ago,
Etched in granite and carved like stone.
She spoke of reveries alive like fire,
Striking and bold and without attire!
She mentioned of dreams in such a soothing tone
That brought comfort to the sick and all those who mourn.
A celebration of words is what she became,
A poet, the poet for some painted name.
She referenced colors of a talented palette
Made from emotions that thundered and galloped.
Words that lie still, like dead graven souls,
And words that stood firm like young readied fouls.
A poet, the poet for some painted name,
Of high points and memories and emotions that pained.
A poet, the poet is music in words,
Celebrating life in the human world.

LOVE IS...

Love is courage. It is surrender.
It is the source of great power,
A strong protector.
It is the light in a darkened realm.
It is bright for all to behold.
Love is sacred and true.
Love exists inside of you.
For its creation is what is seen
In ancient ways, and all it has been
Has broken forth life amidst the veil
Has struck through strife and set sail
For all that love has prevailed.
It is mine, and this is yours.
It's time to open the doors.
And so it is, beloved I am.

THE KEEP

Break down these walls of iron and ash
Blackened by fire of a tumultuous past
Tear down these barricades of cement and stone
The ego bulwark built that retains me alone
Create inroads of compassion and love
May ways in the maze of stone
The byzantine briar of roads
And still, I know
In the crags of rocks that grow
Out from the stone
The tree of life
Break open from strife
And give forth life
You have been imprisoned too long.

YOU

In my dreams, I dream of a lover.
In my heart, I love no other.
For all the spontaneous things you do
Have me constantly thinking of you.
Everywhere I see your face.
For every time, song and place.
In the moment that you glimpsed my world,
I never felt alone again.
For all my dreams came unfurled
When I put my trust in you, my friend.

COUNTING THE WAYS

How much do I adore thee?
Let me count the ways.
As infinite as the starlight sky
Or the drops of water down a mountain creek.
How many leaves can you count on a tree?
Or how many turns exist in an infinite maze?
The story unfolds in a babbling brook.
It whispers in the breeze wild and forsook.
It creeps in the ground with Mother Earth's beat.
It sweeps in the sounds and rhythms repeat.
The intensity of breath, our God-given source.
The immensity of myths and legends foretold.
It's the shine of the sun and of a king's crown.
And beseeches the vagabond on common ground.
It's the warmth of a lover's touch, the sound of a lark.
It's everything that means so much when love is embarked.
And this is what it means when the ships mast unfurls.
It's the voyage of time in every nook and curl.
It's the gentle embrace of heaven's gate.
The welcoming arms lovers satiate.
It's the pros and the cons,
It's the rights and the wrongs.
It's the entirety of the yin and yang.
It's the divine roles in the turn of tides,
And it's my destiny to maintain.

ARGUMENTS AND AGREEMENTS

It's a shame to see people walk away
With pride in their hearts and selfish dismay.
It hurts to see someone walk out of the house,
Leaving behind the pain of a spouse.
Oh, how it brings a tear to my eyes
To think such a division a family couldn't despise.
And with such joy that was shown just moments ago,
I guess there are things we will never understand or know.

A BREAK OF LIGHT

The heaven draped with stars line a glistening sky
As birds of prey wave, their wings flash by.
The trees that tower, all windblown and torn,
Echo the call of a churning mourn.
The fog rolls in and listlessly plays
Among the waters dark and stark gaze.
The animals that play so quietly along the river
Fill the breeze with acrid shivers.
As if a spirit tried to tell
The tale of the old wishing well.
In amber fields, on moonlight nights,
Under starlight skies bedazzled in white diamonds.
The darkness remains a veil which covers the land
And plots to overpower with a frightening hand.
Just when the forest fills with shadows from the moon,
A feeling arises that something will happen soon.
A break of light hits the fiery night
With colors of a bloody rose
The sun arises, the corona is seen
As the night sleeps and goes.

THE COMING OF SPRING

Winter's breath now fades away
As spring is in the air
The arrival of it has come today
With the hope of weather fair.

The crocuses poke their sleepy heads
Through the winter's last fallen snow
And linger on the dainty stems
Upon the earth below.

The budding trees awaken
With prideful glory seen
And blossom with a lacy fashion
Its fancy flowers gleamed.

Oh, happy spring! Oh, happy day!
The daffodils have come to play
The tulips laugh with earth's delight
In the coming of spring's fearsome sight.

GRATITUDE

Your simple acts of kindness have
Touched my heart in many ways
So much so I am speechless to give
This gratitude of many days.

I know my life is richer for
Knowing you and your galore
For all that you stand for
This gratitude in my heart.

Your example of unselfish love
This serviced life brought from above
And so, I sing out with song
The jubilance in hands of spades
You've touched my heart in many ways.

THE SECRET DOOR

A secret door, locked and untouched,
Lies in the corner of a shadowy hutch.
It has but one key, which has not been used
But twisted and torn and fragile and bruised.
Inside the windows peer, colors so bright
That glow, oh so dimly in the mystical light.
If perception gave way to see all the way through,
Wonderful things could happen to you!
The colors would dance with dreams and of love
That long for the time you will rise above.
That withered key that lies in your hands
To open the door that firmly stands.
Then the colors inside would turn to you
Along with this world I built for two.
To share all my dreams of this shadowy hutch
Would unlock the fear that imprisoned my clutch.
Let my colors free, and you shall find
That this love I fear will be both yours and mine.

OLD MAN WINTER

Words fell from his lips
Like featherweight snowflakes
Crystalized in the wind
And the gentle sway of grey trees
Play upon his mountain brow
The air sank to the earth
Heavy with snow as
Winter rolls
Its windswept words
Falling from his lips
Of old man winter's world.

About the Author

Nicole Personette was born in a small town of New England known as the Gateway to Cape Cod. Her ancestry is part of the Mayflower Society and the Daughters of the Revolution. She follows the family tradition of poets including her grandmother Ruth Caswell, who wrote for the local newspaper, as well as a beloved American literary figure, Henry Wadsworth Longfellow. She has performed live for the American Poets Society in Anaheim California, has been invited to Las Vegas and enjoyed performances in her local town of Charlottesville Virginia for the Bridge Performing Arts Center. She in in contact with the SWAG group for literary performances and enjoyed sharing her work at the French Press Coffee Shop of Waynesboro, Virginia. She has been published by the Women's Initiative of Charlottesville's Challenge to Change Essay Contest and has worked with the Charlottesville's Writers Group. Her artistic venue took on a new role when completing a residency at Ligmincha International's Bon Buddhist retreat to include esoteric and deeply spiritual subjects in her poetry. She researches metaphysical and cultural knowledge and enjoys putting complicated subjects into simplistic form. So inspired the name of the book, *The Dakini Codex*. Included is a compilation of her work spanning her lifetime and starting from publications from high school literary magazines to published work in a former Nantucket bed-and-breakfast known then as the Century House. All is a journey of a lifetime, taking in measures of moments capturing scenes with words like a snapshot of a photograph. It has been her pleasure to use this creative measure to teach others.

www.ingramcontent.com/pod-product-compliance
Lightning Source LLC
Chambersburg PA
CBHW061345160726
47995CB00001B/186